THE EYE OF THE WHALE

A Rescue Story

Jennifer O'Connell

TILBURY HOUSE, PUBLISHERS · GARDINER, MAINE

TILBURY HOUSE, PUBLISHERS
103 Brunswick Avenue
Gardiner, Maine 04345
800–582–1899 • www.tilburyhouse.com

First hardcover edition: May 1, 2013 • 10 9 8 7 6 5 4 3 2 1

For Lulu Delacre, Susan Stockdale, and Janet Morgan Stoeke—with love and gratitude for your invaluable assistance
with this book. And in memory of Ruby, my loyal companion for fourteen years. —JO'C

A portion of the author's proceeds from the sale of this book goes to support the work of The Marine Mammal
Center in Sausalito, California, www.MarineMammalCenter.org.

Library of Congress Cataloging-in-Publication Data
O'Connell, Jennifer, 1956-
  The eye of the whale : a rescue story / Jennifer O'Connell. — First hardcover edition.
     pages cm
  Audience: K to grade 3.
  ISBN 978-0-88448-335-9 (hardcover : alk. paper)
 1. Humpback whale—California—San Francisco—Juvenile literature. 2. Wildlife rescue—California—
San Francisco—Juvenile literature. I. Title.
  QL737.C424O26 2012
  599.5'25—dc23   2012031165

Designed by Geraldine Millham, Westport, Massachusetts
Printed and bound by Sung In Printing Ltd., Dang Jung-Dong 242-2, GungPo-si, eKyunggi-do, Korea; March 2013

*T*hrough the morning fog, a fisherman sees trouble.

It's a whale—tangled in the lines from crab traps.
"Whale in distress!" he calls into his radio.

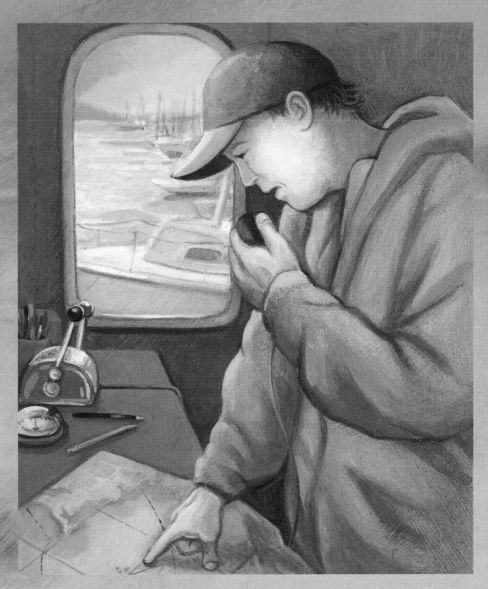

Back on shore a captain answers the call.
"We're on it," he says.

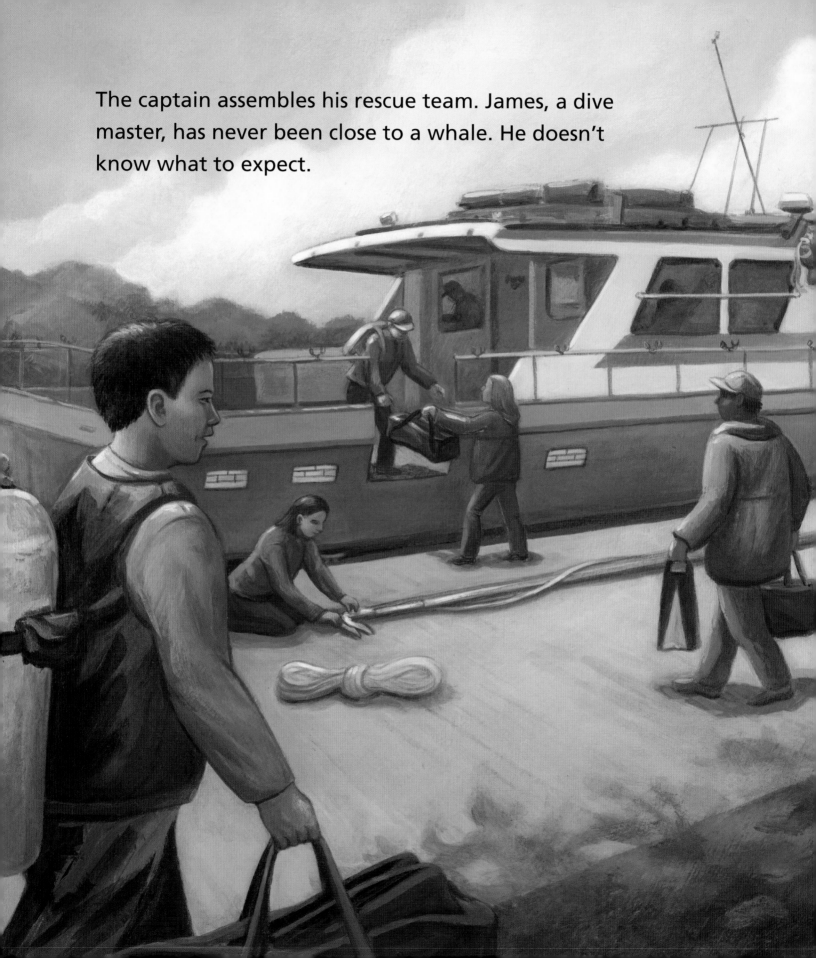

The captain assembles his rescue team. James, a dive master, has never been close to a whale. He doesn't know what to expect.

They might not reach the whale in time.
Sharks could find it first.

When they reach the reported location, there is only a sea lion, bobbing in the waves. Then a puff of mist shoots up. The captain speeds over.

The whale is floating, not moving. It is huge, most likely a female. "Can't see much below the surface," says the captain. James puts on his flippers.

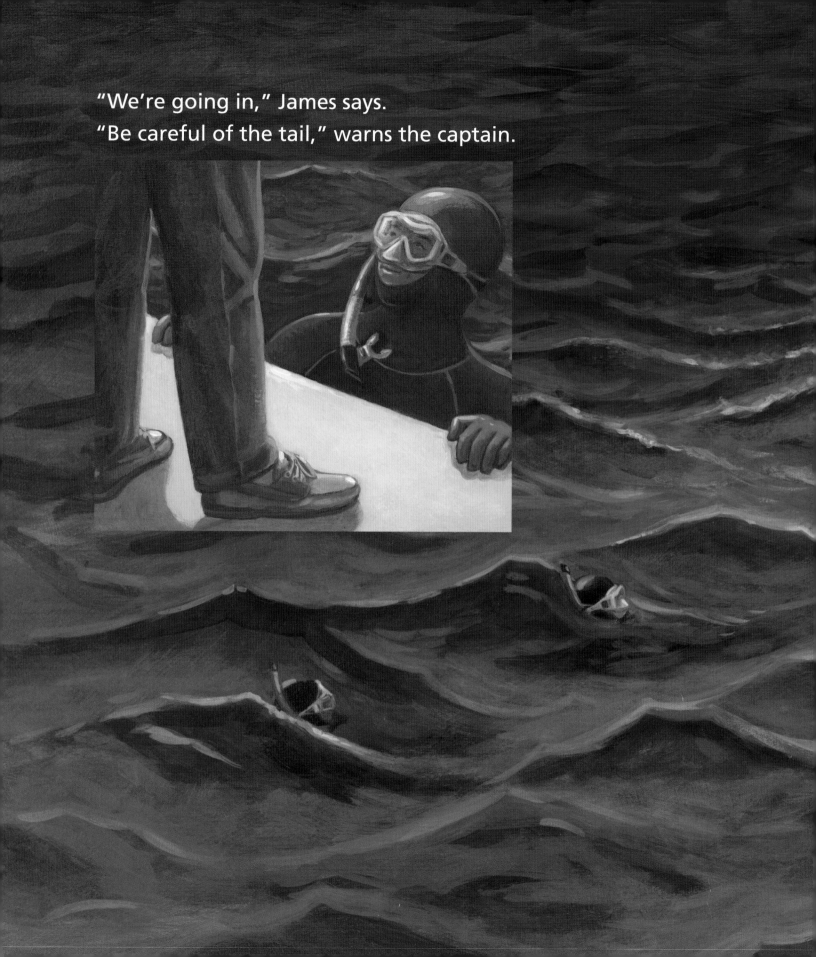

"We're going in," James says.

"Be careful of the tail," warns the captain.

The divers rise and fall with the dark swells.
Water churns as the whale rolls to her side.

An eye slowly surfaces and looks at James.
Then a giant flipper appears and James
knows to stay back.

The whale rolls down again and James swims
to her side. He sees lines cutting into her skin.
He takes a deep breath and dives.

There are scores of ropes trapping the whale.
She is barely able to breathe.

The divers race back to the boat.
"We have to cut the lines or she'll die!" James shouts.

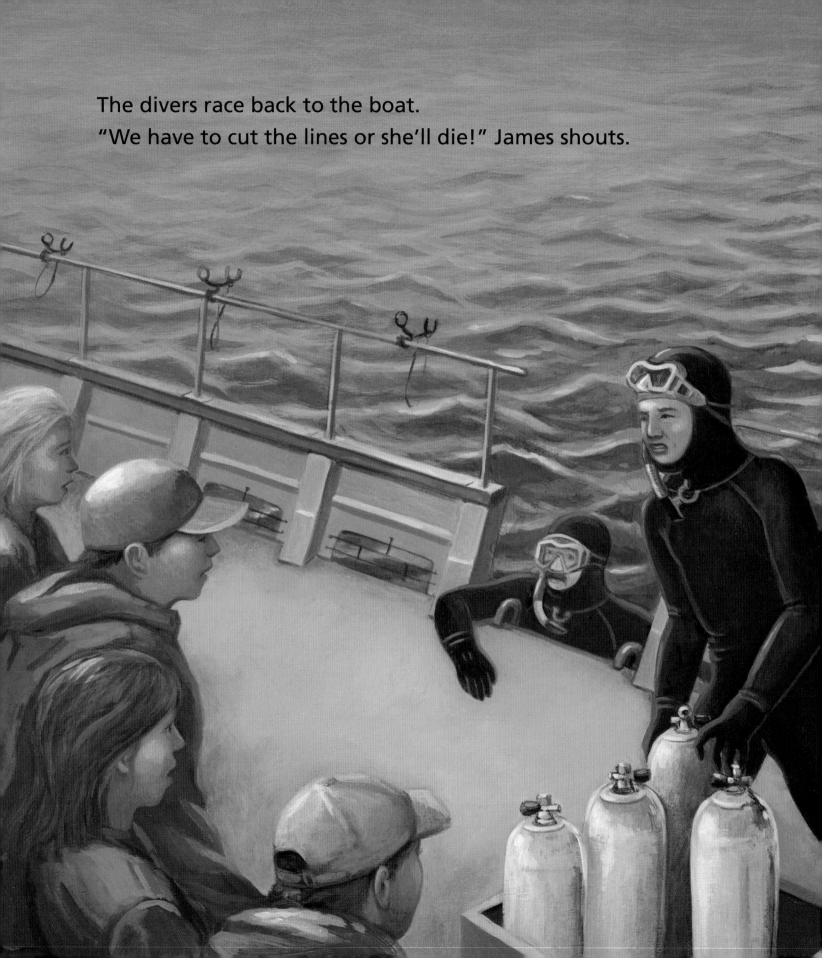

"She swims with her tail, so we'll cut those lines last. If the whale starts moving, get out of the way!"

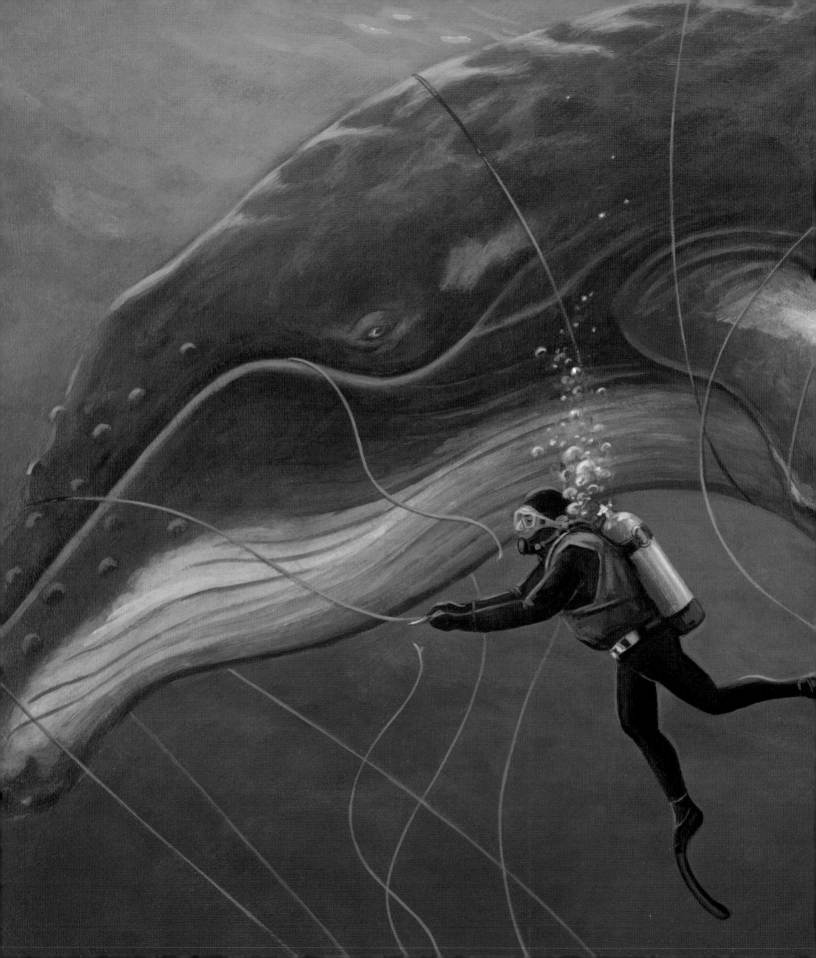

The divers work to save her,
cutting one line after another.

The whale watches everything James does.

Finally, the last line is cut and the whale drifts down into the deep water.

"We did it!" The divers scan the ocean for movement. They know the whale must come up to breathe. James wonders where she has gone. Then a loud humming sound vibrates through the water.

And they see her. The whale whirls
around the divers in a fast, wild dance.
Then she disappears. James is puzzled.

With a jolt, James sees her heading straight for him!

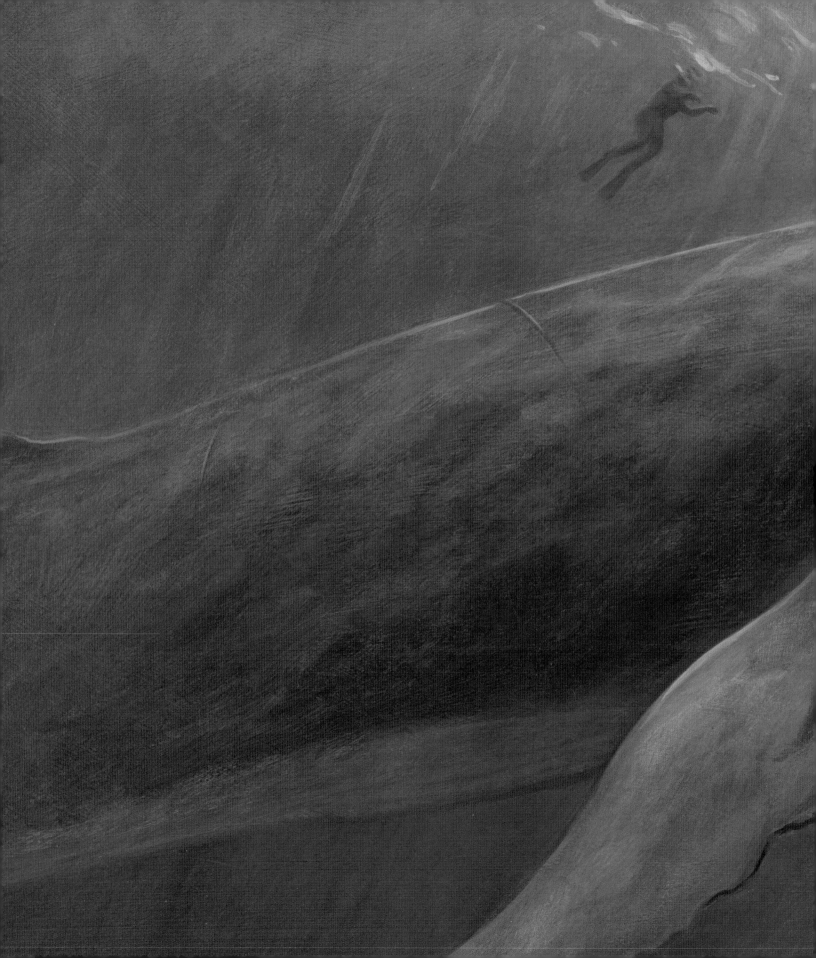

The whale pushes him, ever so gently, a little nudge.
Then, one by one, she nudges the other divers, too.

She looks at James with her beautiful eye.
And plunges back into the dark sea.

ON THE MORNING OF DECEMBER 11, 2005, FISHERMAN RYAN TOM CAME UPON A 50-FOOT-LONG HUMPBACK WHALE TANGLED IN CRAB-TRAP LINES ABOUT 18 MILES OFF THE COAST OF SAN FRANCISCO.

He called Captain Mick Menigoz, who then called The Marine Mammal Center, an organization that helps mammals that live in the ocean. The rescue crew rushed to Captain Mick's boat, *Superfish,* and they set off to see what could be done.

When the crew found the whale, she was barely able to keep her blowhole above the surface to breathe. Hundreds of yards of tangled lines and heavy crab traps were anchoring the whale down to the ocean floor. Realizing how hard it would be to cut lines from on board the boat, divers James Moskito, Tim Young, Jason Russey, and Ted Vivian went into the water to cut them. They were risking their lives to do it, since one quick move of a whale's tail can kill a person (which, sadly, has occurred in the past). Others on board *Superfish* included Dr. Frances Gulland, DVM, Jim Smith, and Kathi Koontz, all from The Marine Mammal Center, as well as crew members Geary Barnes and Holly Drouillard. The story quickly spread and has been celebrated around the world.

As people found out about the event, questions arose. Did the whale help the divers by staying still and calm as they cut the lines or was she just exhausted? Was the whale full of joy after being freed or did she swim in circles to stretch out her huge body after being tied up for so long? How do we explain the whale nudging all the divers, then looking directly at each of them?

Research on whale brains suggests that whales may have the ability to experience emotions. We don't know what this particular whale was feeling. What we do know is that the rescue had a great emotional impact on the divers, who have said that when the whale swam up to them and nudged them, it was one of the most fantastic moments of their lives.

• • •

I thank James Moskito who was so generous in giving his time to tell me his story. I also thank Mick Menigoz for kindly allowing me to go on his boat, *Superfish,* to the Farallon Islands. Thanks also to Kathi Koontz for sharing further details on the rescue.

• • •

Humans continue to kill whales with hunting, pollution, boat propellers, fishing lines, nets, and sonar. However, if we choose to respect and protect these magnificent creatures, they will continue to live and inspire future generations.

• • •

For suggestions on using this book in the classroom, please visit the webpage for *The Eye of the Whale* at www.tilburyhouse.com and click on "Teachers Take Note" at the bottom of the page.